Mysterious Encounters

Cities of Gold

by Shirley Raye Redmond

KIDHAVEN PRESS
A part of Gale, Cengage Learning

GALE
CENGAGE Learning™

Detroit • New York • San Francisco • New Haven, Conn • Waterville, Maine • London

© 2010 Gale, Cengage Learning

Every effort has been made to trace the owners of copyrighted material.

LIBRARY OF CONGRESS CATALOGING-IN-PUBLICATION DATA

Redmond, Shirley-Raye, 1955-
Cities of gold / by Shirley Raye Redmond.
   p. cm. -- (Mysterious encounters)
Includes bibliographical references and index.
ISBN 978-0-7377-5036-2 (hardcover)
1. Geographical myths. I. Title.
GR940.R44 2010
398.23'4--dc22
                                                                    2009044585

KidHaven Press
27500 Drake Rd.
Farmington Hills, MI 48331

ISBN-13: 978-0-7377-5036-2
ISBN-10: 0-7377-5036-7

Printed in the United States of America
1 2 3 4 5 6 7 14 13 12 11 10

Printed by Bang Printing, Brainerd, MN, 1st Ptg., 05/2010

Contents

Chapter 1

The Lure of Gold

Kingdoms of power and great riches have long sparked the imaginations of people around the world. Over the centuries, adventurers have sought the lost city of Atlantis and the mysterious kingdom of Ophir, where King Solomon is said to have obtained the gold, gems, and ivory for his temple in Jerusalem.

In 1145, Bishop Hugh of Syria visited Rome. He informed the Pope about a powerful Christian king named Prester John, who ruled that lands beyond Persia—or so the bishop had been told. "He enjoys such great glory and wealth that he uses no scepter save one of emerald,"[1] the bishop said.

Europeans were at once fascinated by the tale.

King Solomon receives gold from the mysterious kingdom of Ophir.

Soon the legend of Prester John grew and spread. It was said that he lived in a crystal palace and slept on a bed decorated with sapphires. For hundreds of years, crusaders and bold explorers hoped to locate this rich kingdom. No one did. Still, the legend endured. In 1295, Italian explorer Marco Polo returned from his travels in Asia. When he declared that Prester John's kingdom did not exist, the people did not believe him. They even accused him of lying!

A drawing of the mythical Prester John. Even though there was no proof of his existence, people strongly believed in his legend and wealth.

In 1497, Portuguese explorer Vasco de Gama mapped the coastline of Mozambique in southeast Africa. He also inquired about the legendary Prester John. Later, he wrote in his logbook: "We were told that Prester John resided not far from this place; that he held many cities along the coast and the inhabitants of these cities were great merchants and owned big ships."[2]

New Life for Old Legends

On October 11, 1492, Christopher Columbus, an Italian explorer sailing for King Ferdinand and Queen Isabella of Spain, landed on an island in the Caribbean. He noted that some of the natives that came to greet him and his men wore little pieces of gold in their noses. They told Columbus about a king to the south of the island, who owned many vessels filled with gold.

Columbus later found gold so abundant in Hispaniola that months later he wrote to the King of

Christopher Columbus

After Columbus's first voyage in 1492, the West Indies were often referred to as the Isles of the Antilles, and the Caribbean Sea was called the Sea of the Antilles.

Spain, "I promise, with such small helps as our invincible Majesties may afford me, to furnish them with all they gold they need."[3] Soon word about this discovery started a gold rush. Bold Spanish soldiers, businessmen, and adventurers made the long and dangerous journey to the New World for, "God, glory and gold."[4]

Many of the **conquistadors** were certain they would locate the fabled Seven Cities of Gold. According to the legend, seven Portuguese bishops fled Europe in the year A.D. 714 to escape the conquering **Moors**. The bishops took their followers with them and escaped in ships. The story goes that they sailed west across the Atlantic Ocean. They found an island named Antillia and established seven Christian cities of great wealth and success. The stories about these cities became more elaborate as they were passed down from one generation to another. Many believed the fantastic stories were true. Those with a longing for gold and adventure made hard and dangerous journeys in hopes of finding those legendary cities somewhere in the New World.

Aztec Treasure and Inca Gold

However, no one ever located the island of the Seven Cities. At first, it didn't matter. There were other rich kingdoms to be found. The Spaniard Hernán Cortés conquered the wealthy Aztecs in Mexico in the year 1521. Assisted by Indian tribes

An ornament thought to be part of Montezuma's treasure. Cortés took the treasure and sent it back to Spain.

who had long been forced to pay **tribute** to the Aztecs, Cortés and his Spanish soldiers marched into the capital city of Tenochtitlan. The city was located on an island in the middle of a lake and had a population of approximately 100,000. The towering temples and large homes glittered like gold in the sun. There were floating gardens. People wore gold and silver jewelry studded with precious gems. The priests and members of the royal family wore elaborate feathered headdresses and beautiful clothes. Cortés claimed Emperor Montezuma's treasure for himself and sent the required one-fifth back to the king in Spain. Some years later, Cortés returned to Spain and died a famous and wealthy man.

In 1532, conquistador Francisco Pizarro conquered the Inca Empire in South America. After stripping 700 sheets of pure gold from the walls of the temple, Pizarro held Emperor Atahualpa for ransom. He demanded that a large room be filled with gold and silver. Overnight, Pizarro became a very wealthy man. After setting aside the required one-fifth for the king, Pizarro rewarded each of his soldiers with a bounty worth 90 pounds of gold and 180 pounds of silver.

Conquistador Francisco Pizarro, right, meeting Inca emperor Atahualpa in 1532.

The Treasure of Gran Paititi

With every new conquest, the word quickly spread that fame and fortune awaited those bold enough to seek it. As soon as Pizarro had his royal captive killed in Cuzco, rumors made their way throughout Peru and beyond that there was still much Inca gold to be had. It was reported that one of Emperor Atahualpa's younger brothers had fled to Gran Paititi, an Inca city of refuge, taking a great quantity of

Inca treasure with him. In the Quechuan language of the Inca, the word *Paititi* means "Home of the Jaguar Father."

It was said this city, decorated with golden statues, was located near a waterfall, hidden in the Peruvian rain forest near Bolivia and Brazil. According to the reports, great quantities of gold, silver, and amber were stored there. It was also reported that inside the city, there was a ceremonial cornfield, which contained silver cornstalks and ears of corn made from real gold.

The conquistadors searched for many years, but no one ever located Paititi. Some said there was no such refuge city, that it was only a rumor or maybe wishful thinking.

Still, the stories circulated and the legend grew. The possibility that it did exist fascinated the Spaniards and others around the world for hundreds of years.

Chapter 2

The Search for Cibola

I n the spring of 1536, Spanish slave traders discovered a small party of starving, ragged men wandering along the northern frontier of Mexico. One of them was a white man, with long hair and a beard that fell to his waist. With him was an African slave named Estevan and some Indians. The slave traders were astonished when the man, speaking fluent Castilian Spanish, told them his name was Alvar Cabeza de Vaca.

He related a long tale of being shipwrecked and enslaved by Indians. He said he and his companions had been marching aimlesslessly across the continent for eight years. Cabeza de Vaca also mentioned incredible tales of rich cities to the north

of New Spain. He referred to them as the Seven Cities of Cibola. He and his companions were then escorted to Mexico City to repeat their account to the **viceroy**.

The Seven Cities of Cibola

The viceroy of Mexico City, Antonio de Mendoza, welcomed Cabeza de Vaca like a long-lost hero. He questioned him closely about the Seven Cities of Cibola. When he asked Cabeza de Vaca if he'd seen the cities for himself, the man admitted truthfully that he had not. He described the land he'd traveled through as "remote and **malign**, devoid [lacking] of resources."[5] Still, Mendoza was intrigued by the tales. He wondered if Cibola was one of the cities founded by the Christian bishops long ago.

Mendoza organized a **reconnaissance** party. He hoped the scouts would find an empire whose wealth would rival that of the Aztecs or Incas. He selected a French **Franciscan friar** to lead the search

Hidden Gold

The fables live on. Treasure seekers say there are 16,000 gold bars stacked against the walls of seven caves *somewhere* beneath Victorio Peak near Las Cruces, New Mexico.

party. Fray Marcos de Niza was a skilled mapmaker and fearless explorer, having accompanied con- quistadors on **expeditions** to Peru and Guatemala. Estevan agreed to serve as a guide.

On March 7, 1539, the two men headed north. They were accompanied by a band of Indian allies. Estevan wore brightly colored robes and a cape. The bells on his wrists and ankles jangled when he walked. He also brought along two hunting grey- hounds. Fray Marcos carried small samples of gold, silver, copper, and iron in the pocket of his long gray robe. He would show these to natives they encountered on the trip.

Five months later, Fray Marcos returned with good news and bad news. He reported that hos- tile Indians had killed Estevan. But they'd found Cibola—or so he believed. He'd spied the great city in the distance and declared that it was big- ger than Mexico City. He also reported that those they'd encountered on the way informed him there was much gold in the city. The natives drank from gold cups and wore gold earrings. They even used sweat scrapers made from gold! Although he toyed with the idea of entering the city, Fray Marcos de- cided that it was instead his duty to return to tell the viceroy about their discovery.

Coronado's Expedition

The news spread like wildfire through the city. Hundreds of men were ready to set out for the

Francisco Vásquez de Coronado led an expedition to find the Seven Cities of Gold. Instead he found seven little villages.

Seven Cities. Mendoza assigned his young aide Francisco Vásquez de Coronado to head up the expedition. Coronado was a nobleman. He was honest, responsible, and hard-working. Coronado was so certain his mission would be successful that he invested 50,000 **ducats** of his own money into the expedition.

Coronado interviewed each applicant who

wanted to make the trip. Every man was paid 30 pesos, provided with necessary equipment, and promised rich land grants. Approximately 300 soldiers were recruited, along with Fray Marcos and several other priests. 800 Indians also were included. Some were warrior allies. Others were servants to cook and do chores. African slaves were brought along to tend the 1,000 head of cattle, sheep, and pigs.

On February 23, 1540, Coronado put on his plumed helmet and **gilded** armor that glistened like gold in the sun. He was excited and eager to explore the region. He was certain he would find a fortune in gold in Cibola.

But the feverish fantasies of fame and fortune didn't come true. The men traveled hundreds of miles and found not a single golden city. With every passing day, the men grew more and more suspicious of Fray Marcos. The food supply dwindled. Many men and horses died because of the harsh conditions.

Then they arrived at what was said to be the first of the seven cities. Coronado found it to be a shocking disappointment. It was nothing more than a crowded village with huts made of red earth. He'd arrived at the Zuni **pueblo** of Hawikuh in what is now the state of New Mexico. Although some of the 800 people there did live in multistoried houses, there was no gold and no goldsmiths or sil-

Coronado's gilded armor, similar to this one, made him a target for the Zunis, who fought the Spanish.

versmiths. The soldiers turned on Fray Marcos and cursed him.

When the Zunis would not swear **allegiance** to the king of Spain, a battle followed. Coronado's gilded armor made him a special target. He was pelted with arrows and rocks. Finally, a boulder knocked him from his horse and he lay unconscious on the ground, protected by his men.

Following the battle, Coronado wrote a letter to Viceroy Mendoza. He sent Fray Marcos back to Mexico City to deliver it. With disgusted disappointment, Coronado wrote: "I can assure you that he has not told the truth in a single thing. The Seven Cities are seven little villages, all within a radius of five leagues."[6] Every settlement rumored to be one of the outlying golden cities proved to be nothing more than another Indian pueblo.

The Quest for Quivira

Coronado and his men continued to travel through-out the American Southwest. They discovered the Grand Canyon, the Colorado River, and the Painted Desert. Some still hoped they would find the legendary cities of gold.

Their hopes were renewed when a Pawnee captive enslaved by the Cicuye Indians told them that he was from a rich land where there was so much gold it could be hauled away by the wagonloads. The Spaniards nicknamed the man El Turco because of his dark skin and high-cheekbones.

El Turco also told Coronado that the chieftain

Coronado, on the white horse, exploring Kansas in 1541. The Spanish searched for the kingdom of Quivira.

of his land took his afternoon naps under a tree decorated with golden bells that jingled in the breeze. Even common people ate from dishes made from gold and used golden bowls and pitchers. The man called his homeland Quivira.

Coronado decided to test El Turco. He showed him several brass trinkets and asked if this was the sort of gold they used in Quivira. El Turco examined the trinkets. He even sniffed them. Then with a snort, he informed Coronado that this wasn't gold at all—"that he knew gold and silver very well and that he cared little for other metals."[7]

Hopeful of discovering the cities of gold, Coronado decided to follow El Turco to Quivira, which is now present-day Kansas. The Spaniards were impressed with the richness of the vast landscape and awed by the enormous herds of humpbacked cattle called bison. Hailstorms shredded their tents and shattered their crockery. Along the way, they met many nomadic tribes living in houses made of

Population Decline

Surprisingly, the region in the American Southwest that Coronado explored was more heavily populated 450 years ago than it is today.

animal hides and grass. When questioned, none of them knew anything about the grand kingdom of Quivira. The natives knew nothing about gold or silver either.

Coronado angrily demanded to know why El Turco had lied to them. The man admitted that he'd plotted with the Cicuye Indians to lead the Spaniards astray on the plains. "Through lack of provisions, their horse would die, they themselves would become feeble and upon their return, the people of Cicuye could kill them easily."[8]

Humiliated and furious, Coronado had El Turco strangled to death. In August 1542, Coronado led his remaining men south for the sad journey home to Mexico City. He would die there in poverty and disgrace at the age of 44.

Chapter 3

The Quest for El Dorado

Even before conquering the Inca capitol of Cuzco in 1533, the Spaniards had heard rumors about El Dorado. The word is Spanish for "gilded one." It referred to both a South American kingdom rich in gold and jewels and the king or chieftain who ruled there. It was said that during special religious ceremonies, the Chibcha or Muisca ruler had his naked body greased with an oily **resin** and was then powdered from head to foot in gold dust. According to the reports, the gilded king made his way to a mountain lake, followed by a parade of warriors wearing feather headdresses and jaguar skins. Musicians played ceremonial tunes on their horns, pipes, and conch shells. Everyone marched to

This painting shows one of the rumors of El Dorado—that the chief covered his body with gold dust from head to toe.

Lake Guatavita with offerings for the goddess who was said to live in the sacred waters.

At the shore, the chieftain stepped onto a sturdy raft made from rushes, or water reeds. Several important chieftains, wearing feathered plumes, gold armbands, and large gold earrings joined him on the raft and paddled it out to the middle of the lake. While the Muisca people tossed gold ornaments and emeralds into the water, their gilded king plunged into the pure mountain water, leaving the powdered gold as an offering.

Gold Fever!

Many of the conquistadors longed to witness this

El Licenciado Gonzalo Ximenes de Quesada descubrio el nuevo Reyna de Granada

Spanish explorer Gonzalo Jimenez de Quesada tried to find El Dorado. Over 700 of his men died on the journey and their search for the city failed.

strange and extravagant ceremony for themselves. One of them was a Spanish lawyer named Gonzalo Jimenez de Quesada. He and his 900 men endured a terrible journey through the jungle hoping to locate El Dorado. Some drowned in flooded rivers. Others were attacked by jaguars and alligators. Bogged down in the swamps, many of the men died from tropical fevers and the bites of poisonous reptiles and insects. Soon their food ran out. Many starved to death. Some ate snakes and lizards and even the leather torn from their horse harnesses. Quesada threatened death to any man who killed a horse for food.

Finally, in 1536, Quesada and his surviving 166 men reached the land of the Muisca. The tribes were at war with one another, and Quesada took advantage of the situation, easily conquering the

Quesada's expedition tried to drain Lake Guatavita, shown here. They hoped to discover hidden gold relics but found nothing.

Draining A Lake

In 1545, the Spaniards tried again to drain Lake Guatavita, using hundreds of slaves equipped with gourd buckets. They lowered it by ten feet, reclaiming only 40 pounds of gold items.

royal capital at Tunja. The Spaniards also took possession of the salt mines and emerald mines. After stealing piles of gold from the city temple, Quesada had his men burn it down. Hoping to find tons of golden relics, the conquerors made an unsuccessful attempt to drain Lake Guatavita.

Quesada later founded the city of Bogotá in the Muisca heartland. This region is now the country of Colombia. Despite the wealth he accumulated as a successful conquistador, Quesada later died penniless and ill from leprosy.

The Journey to the Cinnamon Country

In 1541, Gonzalo Pizarro, the governor of Quito, Peru, and the younger brother of Francisco Pizarro, who'd conquered the Inca, also led an expedition in search of the fabled Gilded King. It became known as the Journey to the Cinnamon Country, for Pizarro and his second-in-command, Francisco de Orellano, also hoped to locate a forest of cinnamon trees. In the 16th century, cinnamon was a rare and valuable spice used for cooking and in medicines.

Together, Pizarro and Orellano set out for the Andes Mountains, with more than 200 Spaniards—half of them on horseback—and 4,000 natives. They also took 5,000 pigs to eat along the way. As they trekked across the lofty mountain ranges, they were chilled by bitter winds. The mountain passes were high and hard to climb. Many men, horses, and hogs fell to their deaths. Once there was a violent earthquake. Choking vapors oozed out through the cracks along the mountain trails.

When the men finally descended into the valley below, they encountered intense tropical heat and six weeks of constant rain with frightening thunder and lightning.

In less than two years, more than half the Spanish soldiers had died, along with 3,000 of the

Colombia

Today, Colombia is the world's major source of emeralds and ninth in the world for gold production.

natives. The starving survivors returned to Quito without gold, glory, or even the precious cinnamon they'd been seeking.

The royal treasurer in Peru described them in his journal as, "nearly naked, their clothes having rotted by the constant rains and torn besides, so that their only covering consisted of the skins of animals worn in the front and behind ... their swords ... were eaten up with rust. Their feet were bare and wounded by thorns and roots and they were so wan and wasted that one could no longer recognize them...they threw themselves upon the food with so much eagerness that they had to be held back."[9]

Sir Walter Raleigh's Bestselling Lie

The Spanish were not the only explorers hoping to locate the elusive golden realm. Portuguese seamen, German knights, and British noblemen also journeyed to South America hoping to discover El Dorado. One of the most famous was an Englishman named Sir Walter Raleigh. He was a friend of Queen Elizabeth I of England.

After traveling down the Orinoco and Caroni rivers, he wrote a book in 1596 titled, *Discoverie of the large, rich and beautifull Empire of Guiana, with a relation of the great and golden citie of Manoa (which the Spaniards call El Dorado)*.

English explorer Sir Walter Raleigh claimed to have seen El Dorado.

The book with the long title became a bestseller. In it, Raleigh claimed to have visited the golden city and witnessed the legendary ceremony for himself. He also claimed that all of the residents of Manoa powdered themselves with gold dust and that they had willingly showed him their rich gold mines. Soon all of Europe was reading Raleigh's book and talking about El Dorado. Clever promoters and con men took advantage of the book's popularity. They

Chapter 4

Treasure Hunters

The legends of cities of gold are now old and mostly forgotten. But many people around the world are still fascinated by the tales of lost treasure cities. In June 1873, a German businessman-turned-**archeologist** discovered treasure and a lost city in Turkey.

Heinrich Schliemann claimed to have located the lost city of ancient Troy. Many were doubtful. They insisted that there was no such city. They said the story of a handsome Trojan prince named Paris who kidnapped beautiful Queen Helen from her Greek husband wasn't true. It was only a myth.

But Schliemann believed the story was true. Ever since he was a boy, he'd been fascinated by the heroic adventures of Hector and Achilles and the romance between Paris and Helen. Using a copy of *The Iliad* to look for geographical clues in Turkey, Schliemann located what he guessed to be the ancient city and started digging. Archeologists and history scholars laughed at him. Schliemann didn't care.

In his book, *Troy and Its Remains,* published in 1874, Schliemann recounts his discovery: "I cut out the Treasure with a large knife, which it is impossible to do without the very greatest exertion and the most fearful risk to my life, for the great fortification wall, beneath which I had to dig, threatened every moment to fall down upon me. But the sight of so many objects...made me foolhardy, and I never thought of any dangers.... My dear wife stood by me ready to pack the things which I cut out in her shawl."[10]

Everyone was amazed when he revealed his sen-

Priam's Treasure

During the final days of World War II, Soviet soldiers looted the museums in Berlin, Germany. They took Priam's treasure and other valuable artifacts back with them to Russia.

sational find of gold and silver cups, copper trays, a variety of jewels made up into beautiful necklaces and earrings, a golden death mask and two gold diadems or crowns—one made up of over 16,000 pieces of gold. Schliemann called it Priam's treasure, after the king of Troy. Soon other would-be treasure seekers, adventurers, and even historians and archeologists began to wonder if there was still a chance to discover their own long-lost cities of gold.

City in the Clouds

In 1911, an American scholar named Hiram Bingham explored Peru, hoping to find the legendary Inca city of Vilcapampa. He hoped too that he might discover the long-lost Inca treasure said to be hidden there from the conquering Spaniards in the 1500s. One day Peruvian farmers led him to a mountain path skimming the rocky Cliffside. Bingham wrote, "Without the slightest expectation of finding anything more interesting than the stone face terraces ... I entered the untouched forest beyond, and suddenly found myself in a maze of beautiful granite houses! Under a carved rock the little boy showed me a cave beautifully lined with the finest cut stone.... To my astonishment I saw that this wall and its adjoining semicircular temple over the cave were as the finest stonework in the far-famed Temple of the Sun in Cuzco."[11]

Bingham had discovered Machu Picchu, now

Archeologists believe that Machu Picchu, seen here, was a royal estate that the Inca King visited.

one of the best-known archeological sites in the world. It is sometimes called The Lost City in the Clouds. At the time, Bingham and some other scholars believed it to be the birthplace of the Inca Empire. Today, archeologists believe Machu Picchu was merely a royal estate. The Inca king retreated there for rest and relaxation with his family, friends and royal attendants.

Although Bingham found many fine Inca artifacts, there was no lost stash of gold or jewelry. However, historians know that Inca royalty used plates and cups made of gold and silver. Because there were no signs of apparent looting at the site, some archeologist think that many valuable objects may still be found at Machu Picchu one day, and the digging continues.

Exploring the Jungles

Bingham's discovery kindled the imaginations of other archeologists, explorers, and treasure seekers around the world. Many thought that since the lost Inca gold was not discovered at Machu Picchu, then the mysterious city of Paititi and its royal treasure were still somewhere in the jungle.

One of them was the famous archeologist and explorer Percy Harrison Fawcett. He is said to be the real-life inspiration for the Indiana Jones character in the movies. In 1925, Fawcett led an expe-

Famous archeologist and explorer Percy Harrison Fawcett disappeared while exploring Brazil. He was never seen again.

Percy Harrison Fawcett's Claim

Fawcett once reported he'd killed a snake that measured 62 feet (19m). The public ridiculed his claim. Scientists have now verified that giant anaconda live in the Amazon jungle.

dition into the uncharted jungles of Brazil looking for what he called the lost city of Z. He and his travel companions disappeared under mysterious circumstances. No one has ever seen or heard from them since.

In 1954, a former Nazi photographer named Hans Ertl moved with his family to Bolivia. He later went on a photographic expedition into the Andes Mountains and along the Amazon River. He claimed to have located the legendary Paititi in the jungles of Bolivia and made a documentary film about the ruins. However, most government officials did not believe him. Others insisted that the task of clearing the jungle to the site would be too costly and the potential rewards uncertain.

American psychologist and explorer Gregory Deyermenjian launched a dozen trips into the jungle between the years 1984 and 2000. Although

German photographer Hans Ertl, left, went on a photographic expedition into the Andes and along the Amazon River.

he has not yet located Paititi, he has documented many Inca ruins and **petroglyphs**. He also discovered portions of the great Road of Stone, which the Inca used to move armies, mail, and trade goods across the empire.

Myth or Reality?

Are there really lost cities of gold hidden in the jungles still waiting to be discovered? Most people say, "Of course not." Others aren't so sure. Inspired by incredible finds like Machu Picchu, many keep looking.

Sometimes even a small artifact can revive the old legends. In 1969, workers clearing a cave in Colombia discovered a figurine of a small golden raft. On the raft was the figure of a king, surrounded by royal attendants. The excited men recognized the figure at once—El Dorado! Today a replica of the El Dorado raft is on display in Bogotá's Museo del Oro, or Gold Museum. More than 25,000 other gold relics are on display there too.

In 2001, an Italian archeologist named Mario Polia announced that he'd discovered a document in Rome dating back to the 1600s. It is apparently a report addressed to Pope Clement VIII from a Jesuit missionary who described a large Inca city decorated with gold, silver, and jewels. The city, called Paititi by the natives living there, was located near a waterfall near Peru's border with Brazil. Today some people believe that Vatican officials have purposely kept the location of the long-lost treasure city a secret.

In 2008, *National Geographic* presented a TV special on "Lost Cities of the Amazon." Using new 21st century technology, scientists have discovered ancient bridges, city plazas, and extensive roads throughout the South American jungles. They are learning that once there were large cities with populations in the thousands. These ancient ruins, swallowed by the jungle, are difficult to get to. Could one of them be the lost treasure city of Paititi? Perhaps. There are adventurous explorers willing to try to find out. But we may never know for sure.

Notes

Chapter 1: The Lure of Gold

1. Quoted in Time-Life Editors, *Mysterious Lands and Peoples*. Alexandria, Virginia: Time-Life Books, 1991, p. 63.
2. Quoted in *Mysterious Lands and Peoples*, p. 66.
3. Quoted in Adolph F.A. Bandelier, *The Gilded Man*. New York: Appleton & Company, 1893, p. 3.
4. Quoted in Time-Life Editors, *The Spanish West*. Alexandria, Virginia: Time-Life Books, 1976, p. 19.

Chapter 2: The Search for Cibola

5. Quoted in *The Spanish West*, p. 27.
6. Quoted in *The Spanish West*, p. 35.
7. Quoted in Doug Preston, *Cities of Gold*. Albuquerque, New Mexico: University of New Mexico Press, 1992, p. 419.
8. Quoted in Preston, *Cities of Gold*, p. 445.

Chapter 3: The Quest for El Dorado

9. Quoted in Bandelier, *The Gilded Man*, p. 62.

Chapter 4: Treasure Hunters

10. Quoted in Peter James and Nick Thorpe, *Ancient Mysteries*. New York: Ballentine Books, 1999, p. 511.
11. Quoted in Richard Burger and Lucy Salazar, *Machu Picchu: Unveiling the Mystery of the Incas*. New Haven, Connecticut: Yale University Press, 2004, p. 24.

Glossary

allegiance: Loyalty or obligation to another.

archeologist: A scholar who studies prehistoric people and their culture.

conquistadors: Spanish soldiers who journeyed to the New World to conquer lands and the native peoples living there.

ducats: Gold coins used by Europeans for trade prior to World War I.

expeditions: Journeys made by a group of people for a specific purpose, such as exploring or hunting, conquest or trading.

Franciscan friar: A brother or member of the religious order of St. Francis.

gilded: Covered with gold or a shiny, gold-like substance.

malign: Bad or harmful.

Moors: Muslim people from North Africa of mixed Berber and Arab descent.

petroglyphs: Carvings or drawings on rock.

pueblo: A village of adobe dwellings made by Southwest native peoples.

reconnaissance: An inspection or exploration.

resin: A sticky substance obtained from certain plants or trees.

tribute: A gift or payment to show respect or admiration.

viceroy: A government official who ruled as the King or Queen's representative.

For Further Exploration

Books

Marc Aronson, *Sir Walter Raleigh and the Quest for El Dorado*. New York: Clarion Books, 2000. A fascinating account of Raleigh's adventures as he risked starvation, disease, and other dangers in pursuit of the golden realm.

Gary L. Blackwood, *Legends or Lies?* New York: Marshall Cavendish Benchmark, 2005. A good source for those curious about the Amazons, lost civilizations, and cities of gold.

Hal Marcovitz, *Francisco Coronado and the Exploration of the American Southwest*. Philadelphia, Pennsylvania: Chelsea House Publishers, 2000. A brisk 57-page account of Coronado's search for the Seven Cities of Gold.

Time-Life Books, *Mysterious Lands and People*. Alexandria, Virginia: Time-Life Books, 1991. Part of a 33-book series called *Mysteries of the Unknown*, this volume examines tales about Prester John, the doomed citizens of Atlantis, and others.

Web Sites

Legends of America (http://www.legendsofamerica

.com/LA-Treasures.html). An intriguing Web site for those interested in learning more about lost gold mines, unclaimed stashes of silver, the Victorio Peak mystery treasure, and many more.

Quest for Paititi (http://www.paititi.com). Learn about the 2004 exploits of explorer Greg Deyermenjian, as he slashed his way through Peru's jungle in search of the long-lost Inca city.

Index

Picture Credits

About the Author

Shirley Raye Redmond is the author of several nonfiction books for children, including *Mermaids, The Jersey Devil,* and *Blind Tom, The Horse Who Helped Build the Great Railroad.* Redmond lives in New Mexico.